Intermediate Multi-key Solos 3

by Jane Smisor Bastien

KJOS WEST • Neil A. Kjos, Jr., Publisher • San Diego, California

PREFACE

The INTERMEDIATE PIANO COURSE is designed to be used after the student has completed Level 4 of the BASTIEN PIANO LIBRARY. In addition, the INTERMEDIATE PIANO COURSE may be used by a student who has completed *any* elementary piano course. This course is a comprehensive, organized program of study consisting of four books per level which may be used simultaneously for best results. The INTERMEDIATE PIANO COURSE is available in grade levels 1, 2, 3, in each of the following books.

- INTERMEDIATE REPERTOIRE
- INTERMEDIATE THEORY
- INTERMEDIATE TECHNIC
- INTERMEDIATE MULTI-KEY SOLOS

INTERMEDIATE REPERTOIRE introduces the student to many factors of each style period: Baroque, Classical, Romantic, and Contemporary. For each period there are descriptions of overall styles (dress, art, architecture), keyboard instruments, various compositions representative of each period, and a list of composers. The music is a combination of master composer works and pieces written by the Bastiens in each style period. Special emphasis is given to providing more accessible pieces in the Romantic style. The teacher may assign pieces from different periods of the Repertoire book at the same time.

INTERMEDIATE THEORY contains written and playing material to coordinate with the Repertoire book.

INTERMEDIATE TECHNIC contains exercises and etudes by the standard composers as well as many new studies by the Bastiens.

INTERMEDIATE MULTI-KEY SOLOS provides a variety of original music by the Bastiens to encourage the student to explore many keys rather than staying in the limited key selection found in master composer works at the intermediate level.

The INTERMEDIATE PIANO COURSE includes the following books:

Intermediate Repertoire 1 (WP105)	**Intermediate Technic 1** (WP111)
Intermediate Repertoire 2 (WP106)	**Intermediate Technic 2** (WP112)
Intermediate Repertoire 3 (WP107)	**Intermediate Technic 3** (WP113)
Intermediate Theory 1 (WP108)	**Intermediate Multi-key Solos 1** (WP114)
Intermediate Theory 2 (WP109)	**Intermediate Multi-key Solos 2** (WP115)
Intermediate Theory 3 (WP110)	**Intermediate Multi-key Solos 3** (WP116)

ISBN # 0-8497-5202-7

CONTENTS

Carnival

Con spirito

JANE SMISOR BASTIEN

f
cresc.
ff
poco rit.
a tempo
f
ff
gliss
8va

Blue Shadows

JANE SMISOR BASTIEN

Moderato

mf
rit.
pp
8va

Suite in Baroque Style

Prelude

Moderato

JANE SMISOR BASTIEN

cresc.
f
dim.
mp
cresc.
rit.
f

Minuet

mp
p
f

Gigue

f
mf
cresc.
f
mf
sfz

Sea Breeze

Moderato

JANE SMISOR BASTIEN

mp
cantabile
D. C. al Coda
8va
Coda
mf
mp
8va
mf
dim. e rit.
mp
8va

Bolero

JANE SMISOR BASTIEN

mf
cresc.
ff
mf
ff
rit.
8va
8va

Theme and Variations

Moderato

JANE SMISOR BASTIEN

Theme

Var. 1

Var. 2

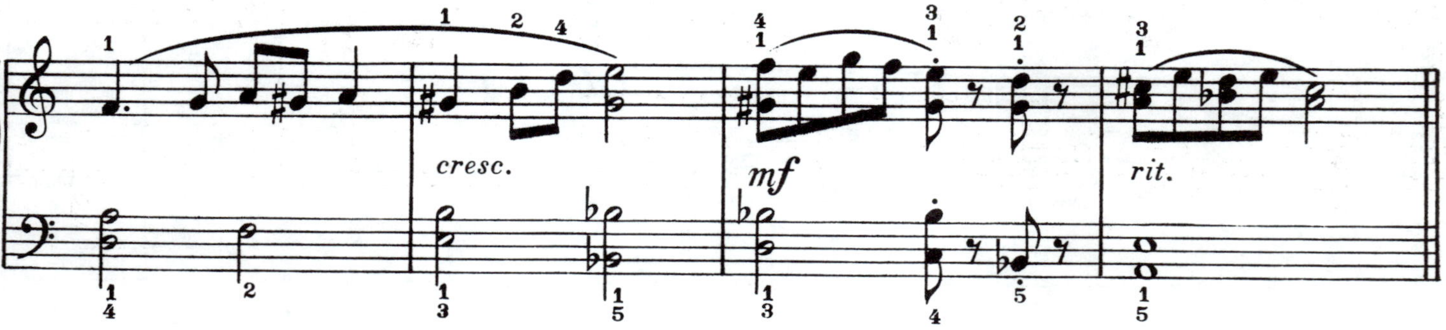

Var. 3

Var. 4

Var. 5

Var. 6
Presto

Chinese Holiday

Con spirito

JANE SMISOR BASTIEN

8va
mf
pp
mf
p
mf
pp poco rit.
a tempo
mf
dim.
rit.
p
a tempo
f

8va
p
8va
mf
mp
8va
f
8va

Night Sounds

JANE SMISOR BASTIEN

Moderato

mp
poco rit.
a tempo
mf cantabile
mf
mp
dim. e rit.
pp

Summer Storm

JANE SMISOR BASTIEN

mf
f
mf
f
mf cresc.
f
ff

Fountains in the Park

JANE SMISOR BASTIEN

Allegro

r. h.
ff
mf
sfz
p
cresc.
f
gliss
8va
8va

Dreamer

JANE SMISOR BASTIEN

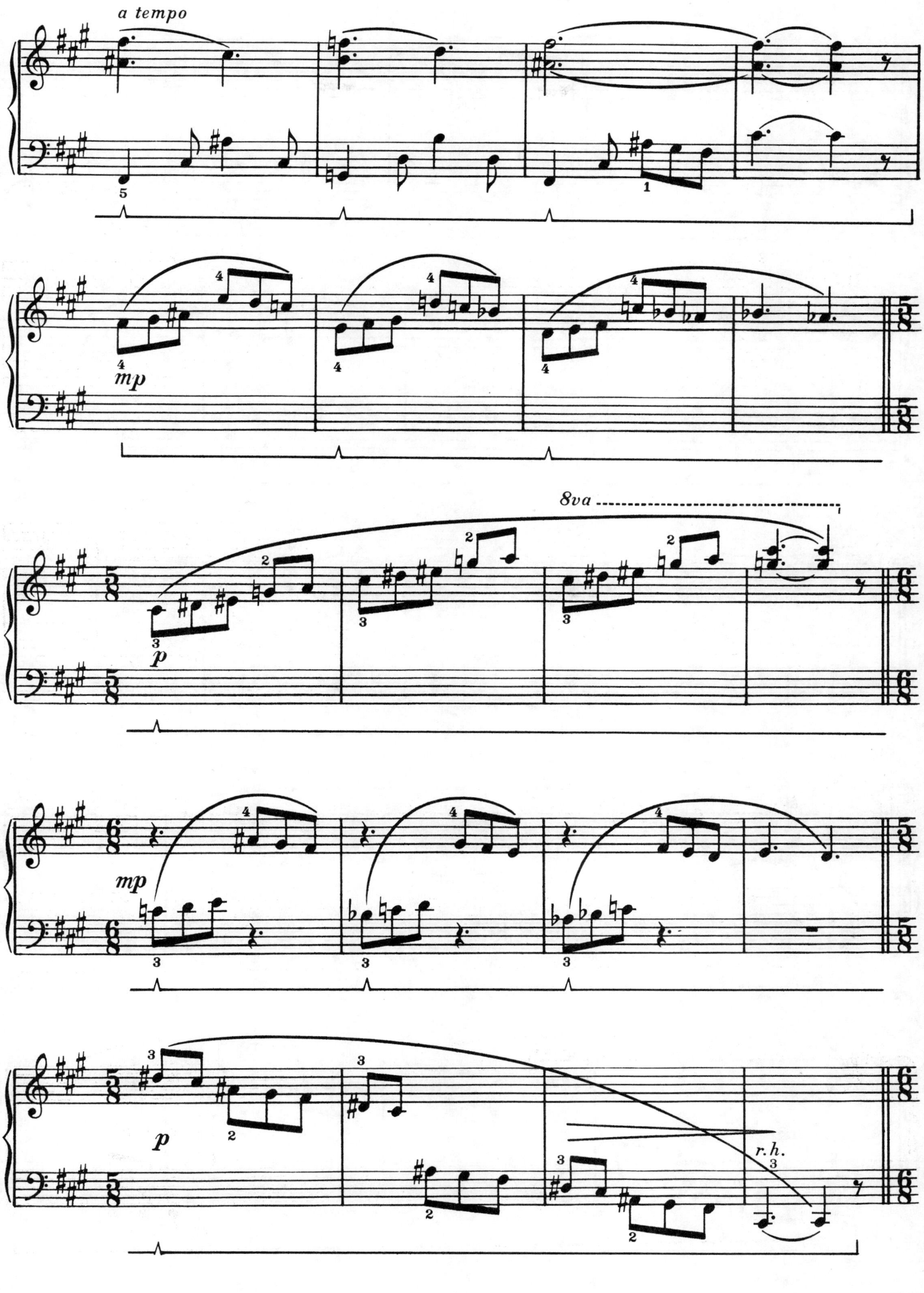
a tempo
mp
8va
p
mp
p
r.h.

mf
mp
poco rit.
pp